PAMPHLETS ON AMERICAN WRITERS · NUMBER 30

UNIVERSITY OF MINNESOTA

Theodore Roethke

BY RALPH J. MILLS, JR.

3437

UNIVERSITY OF MINNESOTA PRESS · MINNEAPOLIS

© Copyright 1963 by the University of Minnesota

ALL RIGHTS RESERVED

Printed in the United States of America at the
Hart Press, Long Prairie, Minnesota

Library of Congress Catalog Card Number: 63-64002

Excerpts from the following poems by Theodore Roethke are used with per-
mission as noted: "Open House," "Orchids," "Frau Bauman, Frau Schmidt,
and Frau Schwartze," "Cuttings, *later*," "The Return," "Where Knock Is Open
Wide," "I Need, I Need," "Bring the Day!" "O Lull Me, Lull Me," "The Lost
Son," "Praise to the End!" "I Cry, Love! Love!" "Four for Sir John Davies,"
"The Heron," "Words for the Wind," "Meditations of an Old Woman," and
"The Dying Man," all from the book *Words for the Wind* by Theodore
Roethke. Copyright © 1958 by Theodore Roethke. Reprinted by permission
of Doubleday & Company, Inc., and Russell & Volkening, Inc. "The Light
Comes Brighter" and "Feud" from the book *Open House.* Copyright 1941 by
Theodore Roethke. Reprinted by permission of Mr. Roethke. "Once More, the
Round." Copyright © 1963 by Hearst Corporation. Reprinted by permission
of *Harper's Bazaar.* "The Minimal." Copyright 1942 by Hearst Magazines,
Inc. Reprinted by permission of *Harper's Bazaar.*

Distributed to high schools in the United States by
McGraw-Hill Book Company, Inc.
New York   Chicago   Corte Madera, Calif.   Dallas

PUBLISHED IN GREAT BRITAIN, INDIA, AND PAKISTAN BY THE OXFORD
UNIVERSITY PRESS, LONDON, BOMBAY, AND KARACHI, AND IN
CANADA BY THOMAS ALLEN, LTD., TORONTO

FOR HELEN

RALPH J. MILLS, JR., has written extensively on modern poetry for periodicals and has contributed to the volume *Poets in Progress*. He is associate chairman of the Committee on Social Thought, University of Chicago.

⤳ *Theodore Roethke*

I̤т ɪs sometimes said of modern poetry that its day is over, that the revolution which swept through all the arts from about 1910 until a decade after World War I died out in the political anxiety and commitment of the 1930's, and that while the great poets who created the modern idiom — Yeats, Eliot, and Pound, for example — pursued their own ways to artistic maturity, writers growing up after them could no longer find the stimulating atmosphere of participation in what Randall Jarrell so aptly called "an individual but irregularly cooperative experimentalism." To a certain extent that view is correct: there has been no concerted poetic movement of real consequence here or in England since the work of Auden, Spender, Day Lewis, and MacNeice in the thirties. Yet even if the excited collective activity inspired by radical and widespread creative ferment gradually dissipated in those years, there was no lack of purpose and talent among the American poets who began to publish notable work near the outset of World War II or the others who appeared soon afterwards.

In his essay "The End of the Line," from which I quoted above, Randall Jarrell acted as a brilliant self-appointed spokesman for his contemporaries, for Robert Lowell, John Frederick Nims, Karl Shapiro, Richard Eberhart, Richard Wilbur, and Theodore Roethke, as well as for himself, when he defined the situation of the younger poet in 1942. "Today, for the poet," he said, "there is an embarrassment of choices: young poets can choose — do choose — to write anything from surrealism to imitations of Robert Bridges; the only thing they have no choice about is making their own choice. The Muse, forsaking her sterner laws, says to everyone: 'Do what you will.' "

The American poets of that generation did exactly what they willed and have produced, without the impetus of any common enterprise other than devotion to their art, a remarkable body of poetry. Ironically enough, they are poets on whom the label of academicism has been fastened occasionally; yet outside of the fact that many of them like Roethke have taught for a living that word, with its pejorative overtones, would seem to have little application. We have academic verse when a poet, instead of learning from the poetic tradition by remaining alive and open to its possibilities in relation to his own gifts and aspirations, submits himself to it automatically or, to change the metaphor, polishes the surface of old conventions. The weakness of the academic writer lies in an acceptance of literature before personal experience and imagination as the source of his art. But the poets I have named, and some not mentioned, showed originality, concern for language, and an abiding honesty toward the facts of their experience. If comparisons with the pioneer writers of twentieth-century modernism do not offer these successors the historical advantage, there is still no doubt in my mind that two or three of the latter can already hold their own surprisingly well in such formidable company.

Of all these later poets Theodore Roethke appears the most considerable, in terms of imaginative daring, stylistic achievement, richness of diction, variety and fullness of music, and unity of vision. From his first book, published in 1941, to the most recent of his poems in the pages of the *New Yorker*, *Sewanee Review*, or *Encounter* he consistently proved himself a poet discontented with the restrictions of a settled manner of composition. This is not to say, of course, that Roethke lacked steadiness or certitude, that he was frivolous or insubstantial; quite the reverse. His poetry

6

grew in distinct stages, each one with its own peculiar qualities and aims, each one expanding and developing from its predecessor, each providing its own special means of furthering the poet's central themes and subjecting them to different modes of apprehension. We should not be surprised then in reading through Roethke's books to discover a wide range of moods and styles: tightly controlled formal lyrics, dramatic monologues and something like an interior monologue, nonsense verse, love lyrics, and meditative poems composed in a very free fashion. His experience reaches from the most extraordinary intuition of the life of nature to lightning flashes of mystical illumination.

To fit Roethke definitely within a given tradition or to link him finally with other poets, past or present, who share certain of his predilections is tempting but too easy. He expressed an affection for John Clare and borrowed the title for his third book from Wordsworth's *The Prelude*, yet he was not drawn to the natural world in quite the same way as either of them, though he maintained affinities with both. Again one might like to proclaim him an investigator of the irrational, a poet obsessed with the pure flow of inner experience, with the preconscious and the unconscious: a poet similar to the young Dylan Thomas or Paul Eluard. Or perhaps he should be classed with the visionary poets he so admired: Blake, Whitman, and Yeats. No doubt every one of these attempts at classification would tell us a partial truth about Roethke, but none would give us the whole of it. He was, in fact, equally at home with any of these other poets, though we will be defeated in the endeavor to read his poetry honestly if we settle for a particular category in which to lodge him and so avoid further thought. Roethke needs first to be seen through his own work.

Behind the profusion of experience we have noted in Roethke's writing one comes upon a preoccupation with the poet's own self

7

as the primary matter of artistic exploration and knowledge, an interest which endows the poems with a sense of personal urgency, even necessity. What do we mean by this self? I think the self, as we shall want to use the word here, can best be called the main principle of the poet's individual life — or for that matter, of any human life — a principle of identity and of being which is generally spiritual in character but also reaches into the realm of the physical. It partakes of what Martin Buber includes in his definition of the "primary word *I-Thou*," which is the speech of a person's entire being in relationship with the other creatures and things of the world, for Roethke viewed the self as continually seeking a harmonious dialogue with all that is. The bulk of Roethke's poetry derives its imaginative strength from the author's restless quest for that communion in which self and creation are joined. Though they take the self as theme we cannot look in these poems for the sort of personal element we associate with the later work of Robert Lowell. Yet they are in their way just as intimate, maybe even more intimate, since some penetrate the protective screen of conscious thought. Lowell focuses often on other personalities, the family, the world of historical time, while Roethke's concentration either is inward, almost untouched by public happenings or by history, or turns outward to the existence of things in nature. But in order to understand his fundamental attachment to this theme of the self we must now look closely at its development within a growing body of poetry.

By any standards *Open House* (1941) is a remarkable first collection of poetry. Roethke's sensitive use of language and his craftsmanship stand out on every page; and if one returns to this book after reading his other work it becomes plain that the author's main interests were already present here. The title poem is a frank announcement of his intention to use himself in some way

8

as the material of his art, but we are not told how. The poem is sharp in its personal disclosure and might justifiably serve as a motto for all of Roethke's subsequent verse:

> My secrets cry aloud.
> I have no need for tongue.
> My heart keeps open house,
> My doors are widely swung.
> An epic of the eyes
> My love, with no disguise.
>
> My truths are all foreknown,
> This anguish self-revealed.
> I'm naked to the bone,
> With nakedness my shield.
> Myself is what I wear:
> I keep the spirit spare.

These sparse, carefully rhymed stanzas characterize Roethke's earlier poetic technique, and their kind is visible everywhere in *Open House*. A certain economy and simplicity of diction, as well as insistent, forceful rhythms, more freely employed as he matured, are in fact lasting trademarks of his style, even though he abandoned some of them almost entirely on occasion in favor of experiments with considerably looser forms. Such departures are especially evident in the long sequence of interior monologues from *The Lost Son* and *Praise to the End* and in the "Meditations of an Old Woman" from *Words for the Wind*, to say nothing of poems later than that. But the experiments are always interspersed, even in recent work, with returns to the simple lyric. Here, as an illustration, is a stanza from "Once More, the Round," which Roethke wrote for his 1962 New Year's greeting:

> Now I adore my life,
> With the Bird, the abiding Leaf,
> With the Fish, the questing Snail,
> And the Eye altering All;

> And I dance with William Blake
> For love, for Love's sake.

The two subjects on which Roethke's imagination most often fastens in *Open House* are the correspondence between the poet's inner life and the life of nature, and the strengths or weaknesses of the individual psyche. Frequently he tries to demonstrate hidden relationships in the processes of both, as in "The Light Comes Brighter," a poem which begins with a very direct account of winter's end and the arrival of spring to a particular landscape:

> The light comes brighter from the east; the caw
> Of restive crows is sharper on the ear.
> A walker at the river's edge may hear
> A cannon crack announce an early thaw.
>
> The sun cuts deep into the heavy drift,
> Though still the guarded snow is winter-sealed,
> At bridgeheads buckled ice begins to shift,
> The river overflows the level field.

The observation and description are quite accurate and undoubtedly derive from the poet's childhood experience of the Michigan countryside. But as in the poetry of Léonie Adams, which Roethke always admired, nature yields a secret analogy with human existence, though it does not appear until the closing lines:

> And soon a branch, part of a hidden scene,
> The leafy mind, that long was furled,
> Will turn its private substance into green,
> And young shoots spread upon our inner world.

Mind and nature are bound in these lines by certain laws and enjoy a common awakening. Still we are left to tease out most of the implications for ourselves because the poet merely hints at the possibilities of this comparison in the present poem. In many of the other poems in this volume Roethke offers further seasonal descriptions but never makes the implied correspondences with

10

human life any more definite than what we have already seen in the lines quoted.

Elsewhere in the book he takes the durability of the mind by itself as artistic material; and in a few poems which show an indebtedness to W. H. Auden (and have never been reprinted) he portrays the opposition to this mental stability through the figures of those victimized by unconscious forces, inherited sicknesses that threaten to destroy psychic balance:

> Exhausted fathers thinned the blood,
> You curse the legacy of pain;
> Darling of an infected brood,
> You feel disaster climb the vein.

These last poems, though they are of little aesthetic interest so far as the bulk of Roethke's writing is concerned, possess some value in foreshadowing the motives behind the tremendous imaginative leap he took in the seven years between *Open House* and *The Lost Son*. For the hostile powers of the unconscious had at last to be dealt with, and are dealt with in the astonishing sequence of interior monologues which record the poet's odyssey through subterranean regions of the psyche, a spiritual journey that remains one of the boldest experiments in modern American poetry. Taken altogether the poems in *Open House* are indicative of Roethke's major themes, but they hardly prepare the reader for the change to an intensely subjective vision in the next book or for the readjustment of his perceptions demanded by this shift. With *The Lost Son* (1948) he emerges as a poet of undeniable originality and stature, whose writing bears its own stylistic signature.

The section of poems with which *The Lost Son* opens may catch by complete surprise the reader who has seen nothing but Roethke's previous work. While emphasis on nature is still maintained attention has now moved away from the earlier images of natural and seasonal activity in the larger sense to a reduced, microscopic

11

RALPH J. MILLS, JR.

scrutiny of plant life that seems almost scientific in its precision but is obviously prompted by the poet's intuition, passion, and sympathy. What in preceding poems would most likely have been a careful description of the outer appearance of a plant or flower becomes an attempt to seize imaginatively the essential life of the flower, as in the haunting "Orchids," where it overlaps ours:

> They lean over the path,
> Adder-mouthed,
> Swaying close to the face,
> Coming out, soft and deceptive,
> Limp and damp, delicate as a young bird's tongue;
> Their fluttery fledgling lips
> Move slowly,
> Drawing in the warm air.

The basis for this sudden alteration in distance and perspective must have been the poet's decision to utilize his close experience in childhood with plants and flowers as substantial matter for his art. However it came about the choice was fortunate because it marked out the route his poetic imagination was to take and, one likes to think, even urged him on his way by revealing the similarities existing between his human life and that of the inhabitants of the plant kingdom which had played so important a part in his youth. Through this new personal vision of the vegetable and mineral, insect and animal, knowledge of which he owed to his boyhood, Roethke found before him the difficult problems of spiritual evolution and the search for psychic identity.

The poet was born in Saginaw, Michigan, in 1908, received his education at the University of Michigan and Harvard, and subsequently taught at Lafayette College, Pennsylvania State University, Bennington College, and for some time at the University of Washington in Seattle, where he was professor of English and poet in residence at the time of his death on August 1, 1963. As a boy he grew up in and around the greenhouses that were the center of

12

the Roethke family's floral establishment, one of the largest and most famous of its time. The business was both retail and wholesale; it was operated by Roethke's father and his Uncle Charlie, aided by a staff of trained florists and also by a working crew of eccentric figures which included the three marvelous old ladies Frau Bauman, Frau Schmidt, and Frau Schwartze, about whom the poet wrote a wonderful and moving elegy that captures the beauty and pleasure of these women at their task. I quote here only a few lines from the first stanza:

> Gone the three ancient ladies
> Who creaked on the greenhouse ladders,
> Reaching up white strings
> To wind, to wind
> The sweet-pea tendrils, the smilax,
> Nasturtiums, the climbing
> Roses, to straighten
> Carnations, red
> Chrysanthemums; the stiff
> Stems, jointed like corn,
> They tied and tucked, —
> These nurses of nobody else.

As a boy Roethke played and worked around these greenhouses. Many of his experiences he transformed elegantly, and often humorously, into poems: we need only look at "Big Wind," "Old Florist," "Child on Top of a Greenhouse," and the poem above to be conscious of that. But from the same intimate knowledge of his father's greenhouses he began those poetic ventures into the scarcely visible — except to the eye of a determined and fascinated observer — motions of plant life that we noticed in "Orchids." In another poem, appropriately entitled "The Minimal," Roethke renders himself in the act of watching:

> I study the lives on a leaf: the little
> Sleepers, numb nudgers in cold dimensions,

13

> Beetles in caves, newts, stone-deaf fishes,
> Lice tethered to long limp subterranean weeds,
> Squirmers in bogs,
> And bacterial creepers
> Wriggling through wounds
> Like elvers in ponds,
> Their wan mouths kissing the warm sutures,
> Cleaning and caressing,
> Creeping and healing.

In the poet's attentive gaze this tiny world increases its size and comes curiously near in its procedures to the one we would like to believe is exclusively man's. Something in the human psyche responds to these minute activities, discovers a mysterious, even terrifying, attraction to levels of existence to which reason or intelligence would quickly assign an inferior value. But an indispensable part of the imaginative breakthrough Roethke achieves in his second book is just this exposure of himself to subrational elements. Thus the disturbing quality in these poems results from the dramatic re-creation of affinities with the lower orders of life, parallels we have banished from thought. And how startling it is for the scientific, technological mind of contemporary man to countenance such images of his origins, of archaic sources of life he shares with lesser forms than himself. If Roethke's endeavors start with a return to his own past experience, the poems surpass the barriers of privacy to delineate hidden patterns in creation; and they accomplish this with a freshness of language and imaginative energy unmatched by any other poet since Dylan Thomas. A poem like "Cuttings, *later*" brings poet — and thus reader — and the newly born plants into a correspondence so delicate and yet profound that there can be only one true conclusion: a kind of psychic rebirth for the poet through his sympathetic contemplation of propagating plants:

> This urge, wrestle, resurrection of dry sticks,
> Cut stems struggling to put down feet,
> What saint strained so much,
> Rose on such lopped limbs to a new life?

> I can hear, underground, that sucking and sobbing,
> In my veins, in my bones I feel it, —
> The small waters seeping upward,
> The tight grains parting at last.
> When sprouts break out,
> Slippery as fish,
> I quail, lean to beginnings, sheath-wet.

Roethke's inclination in these poems to reveal a deep and permanent tie between the "minimal" world of flowers, plants, and small creatures he so benevolently scrutinizes and the inner world of man prepares for the sequence of experimental monologues, the first of which appear in the last section of *The Lost Son* and which are continued in *Praise to the End* (1951). The sequence poems are, so far as I know, unique in modern literature. Undoubtedly they owe their inspiration to the poet's pursuit of the correspondences just mentioned and to the fact that his previous work keeps insisting on such an immersion in the prerational and unconscious areas of experience in the hope of bringing unity to the self and gaining a new harmony with creation.

The poems are grouped around an associational scheme, as Roethke once suggested, and seem closer perhaps to certain experimental tendencies in the modern novel, such as stream of consciousness, than they do to the efforts of most contemporary poets. "Each poem" — there are fourteen in all — "is complete in itself," Roethke says in his "Open Letter" from *Mid-Century American Poets*, "yet each in a sense is a stage in a kind of struggle out of the slime; part of a slow spiritual progress; an effort to be born, and later, to become something more." The poems treat portions of a spiritual journey undertaken by a child-protagonist, a journey

15

the narrative of which does not develop in a direct, logical manner
because it is viewed internally through the fluid movements and
reactions of the protagonist's mind. This protagonist, through
whom we comprehend whatever happens in the poems, plays a
double role: he is both a mask for the poet and a universal type,
any man, for Roethke is at pains to avoid the limitations of a
totally personal significance in the experience created by this
poetic sequence. The journey, while it is basically psychic and
spiritual, also has similarities with quest myths: the hero's descent
into the underworld of the self; a series of ordeals he must pass
or an enemy to be vanquished; his victorious return to familiar
reality, which is now changed by his efforts. This sort of parallel
will make it clear at once that while Roethke's primary intention
is the "struggle for spiritual identity" (his phrase) in the individual
protagonist, that struggle symbolizes a more general body of human experience. This last dimension is, however, implied rather
than heavily outlined through a detailed system of allusion.

In several of the poems we have seen from *The Lost Son,* as well
as in a number of others that cannot be discussed here, Roethke
presses back toward the very beginnings of existence in his concentration on the life process of plants. This practice by itself is suffi-
cient to separate his interests from his contemporaries' and to
display his genuine innovation. Roethke wishes in these poems
to uncover through his imagination the laws of growth in a flower
and relate them to the development of the human self, though it
is done metaphorically rather than scientifically. But short lyric
poems are ultimately unsatisfactory as vehicles for such ambitions
because they are not flexible enough and do not readily permit
the singular approach to experience the poet now envisages. What
he is aiming at is a poetic "history of the psyche" (his phrase)
which opens with the earliest stages of life and traces the evolution
of the spirit in its ordeal of inner and outer conflicts, its desire for

16

"unity of being," to borrow a term from Dante by way of Yeats, that final condition of grace which is a harmony of the self with all things. In Roethke's later work the love of man and woman is involved in this idea of unity and so is an awareness of the Divine. Yet the protagonist's route in the poems is anything but easy, for regressive instincts, desires to remain on the lowest plane of existence or to become a lump of inanimate matter, war upon the natural impulse to growth. The spirit tries to release the self from these destructive attractions and to rise toward the full embrace of life. Nature is the context in which the individual assumes at last his rightful identity, finds love, and engages the spirit in further encounters. Roethke depicted some of the terrors and humiliations attending this venture into buried regions in a poem entitled "The Return":

> A cold key let me in
> That self-infected lair;
> And I lay down with my life,
> With the rags and rotting clothes,
> With a stump of scraggy fang
> Bared for a hunter's boot.

ˣThe self-imposed, and no doubt personally necessary, journey on which the poet sets forth with the first poem of the sequence (as rearranged by Roethke in the order he wishes in *Words for the Wind*), "Where Knock Is Open Wide," immediately alters ordinary spatial and temporal dimensions. Spatial because the poems view a secret landscape of the inner self that resembles the external world only in fragmentary details supplied by memory or momentary perceptions, and these are heightened, distorted, or transfigured, as in a dream, by the various struggles of the spirit in its search for freedom and unity. Temporal because the poet, or the projection of himself which is the protagonist, needs to go back to his childhood experience so that he can relive this evolu-

17

tionary process in writing about it. Thus we witness the activity of the poems from the standpoint of the poet-protagonist himself.

It has already been suggested that these poems carry echoes of archetypal patterns from other modes of experience, particularly mythical and religious. Because the protagonist travels into the regions of memory, the preconscious and the unconscious, he shows distinct similarity to the heroes of myth whom Jung saw as representative of the quest for psychic wholeness. Like those fabulous heroes or the lesser ones of fairy tales Roethke's lone protagonist must endure the trials and dangers of a mission into the darkness of personal history. The prize to be won is rebirth and illumination, what is called in one of the poems "a condition of joy."

x The title of "Where Knock Is Open Wide" is taken from Christopher Smart's poem of praise and celebration, "Song to David," LXXVII, but Roethke's piece, which presents the sensations and thoughts of earliest childhood, seems to use the line from Smart to imply birth and entry into the world. From this aspect Roethke's poem somewhat resembles Dylan Thomas' "Before I knocked," which describes experiences of a child (in this case, Jesus) in the womb. Indeed, Thomas is probably the only one of Roethke's immediate contemporaries who also investigates successfully the fluid exchange of past and present within the self. Roethke establishes his atmosphere with childish perceptions:

> A kitten can
> Bite with his feet;
> Papa and Mamma
> Have more teeth.

He goes on in a few lines to what appears to be an image of birth:

> Once upon a tree
> I came across a time . . .

The tree is a species of the common symbol of the Tree of Life, and the next line recalls the protagonist's introduction to time. A stanza further on we learn the nature of the journey and something of its method:

> What's the time, papa-seed?
> Everything has been twice.
> My father is a fish.

This brief passage draws the protagonist back toward the instant of his conception and fixes our attention on the movement into his personal past, which is a reversal of the temporal order. The middle line makes plain the fact that the poet is not simply rendering the original stages of development in a fictional individual but reliving them in himself to interpret their meaning. We seem to hear the voices of the protagonist and the poet blending in this line. The identification of the father with a fish has again a double reference: first, in allusion to a fishing trip of the father and son, bits of which are given later; second, in hinting at the evolutionary scheme emphasized previously. This process of evolution we witness in the protagonist is universal and leads away, as Roethke writes in his "Open Letter," from "the mire," where "man is no more than a shape writhing from the old rock." In the third section of the poem he sounds the same theme by employing the word "fish" once again, but now as a verb instead of a substantive. This change marks a step forward from domination by an image of ancestry among the lower forms of life to an active desire on the protagonist's part for self-completion:

> A worm has a mouth.
> Who keeps me last?
> Fish me out.
> Please.

Since our point of observation is located within the protagonist's mind, though not at the level of reason or calculation, certain external facts such as his changing age are not always easily determined. We gather, however, that the poems extend over a period from early childhood into late adolescence. Roethke's associative technique allows him to shift back and forth freely in the history of his protagonist, and so he can bring his artistic weight to bear on the themes which matter to him without particular regard for the consistency of linear time. The present poem ranges from the first years of life with their scraps of nonsense verse and nursery songs, through a brief section touching on the small boy's religious emotions, then his fishing trip, and ending with the initial signs of anxiety and guilt which accompany the feeling of desolation caused by the father's death. The narrative progression of the poems, if we may thus speak of it, depends upon Roethke's concern for the advances and setbacks of the evolving spirit.

The loss of his father empties the protagonist's world of its paternal image of God as well:

> Kisses come back,
> I said to Papa;
> He was all whitey bones
> And skin like paper.
>
> God's somewhere else,
> I said to Mamma.
> The evening came
> A long long time.

The last two lines predict a period of deprivation and loneliness to come. And in the next poem, "I Need, I Need," with its title so sharply indicative of the child's terrible hunger for affection and stability, he alternates between a search for the mother:

> A deep dish. Lumps in it.
> I can't taste my mother.

solitude and melancholy:

20

> Went down cellar,
> Talked to a faucet;
> The drippy water
> Had nothing to say.

and a final resort to the diversion of children's habits, rhymes, and games:

> A one is a two is
> I know what you is:
> You're not very nice, —
> So touch my toes twice.

But, clearly enough, these diversions exhibit the inner divisions and turmoil of the protagonist, too. In later sections of the poem a gradual easing of tensions occurs, succeeded by intimations of human possibility and of an abiding kinship with physical creation: "Hear me, soft ears and roundy stones! / It's a dear life I can touch." The poem finally closes by emphasizing two of the traditional four elements thought to compose the universe, water and fire:

> I said to the gate,
> Who else knows
> What water does?
> Dew ate the fire.

Here the gate symbolizes all that prevents the protagonist from rebirth into the world, from the potential of his existence. Like beings, objects, and places in fairy tale and folklore, creatures and things in Roethke's poetic cosmos are invested with magical properties, can hinder or help the spirit in its growth. Thus the protagonist seeks the true way by asking questions in this subterranean and animistic kingdom from which he must obtain new life or sink back into the "dark pond" — as Roethke calls the deep unconscious — where oblivion awaits him. The water mentioned in the passage above should not, however, be identified with that sinister place; rather it signifies a continuation of the journey into daylight, the constant will of the self to accomplish, in Robert Frost's words, this "serial ordeal."

Dew consumes one fire in this same stanza only to disclose another kind in the next. The first should probably be understood as the fever of discord in the protagonist, while the second, which appears momentarily in the poem's final lines — "I know another fire. / Has roots." — surely is meant to remind us of fire's ancient use as a symbol of spirit. So we realize that the entire movement of the first two poems in the sequence constitutes an ascent from origins, from the introduction to death, the experience of fear and isolation, to the recognition of freedom and possibility beyond present conditions, though such prospects are never mistaken for a guarantee of security. Life, as it is seen in Roethke's poetry, can best be defined as always becoming.

"Bring the Day!" fulfills the promise of spiritual progress implied before. It is a celebration of self and nature together in a newly won relation, and as such it marks the conversion of the haunted landscape of unknown terrors and hidden demons projected by the self into the radiant external world of insects and birds, grass and flowers. The poem begins with an exuberant burst of song which sounds as if Roethke might have had both John Lyly and Edward Lear in mind when he wrote it:

> Bees and lilies there were,
> Bees and lilies there were,
> Either to other, —
> Which would you rather?
> Bees and lilies were there.

This mood of celebration, of self-possession and joy, prevails throughout the poem. Nature guides the protagonist further along the path he must travel and hints in symbols which recall those of "I Need, I Need" at the pattern of his journey from confinement to fluidity: "The grass says what the wind says: / Begin with the rock; / End with water."

The third and concluding section shows the emergent self in the image of a tiny bird waking to existence, feeling a little its own possibilities, and facing a life that has cast off its ties with the past and only looks forward. The gentle lyricism of the stanza again points up Roethke's uncanny sensitiveness to the subtlest details of nature and their covert human meanings:

> O small bird wakening,
> Light as a hand among blossoms,
> Hardly any old angels are around any more.
> The air's quiet under the small leaves.
> The dust, the long dust, stays.
> The spiders sail into summer.
> It's time to begin!
> To begin!

Following this poem three others, "Give Way, Ye Gates," "Sensibility! O La!" and "O Lull Me, Lull Me," lead up to "The Lost Son," which is the key poem of the sequence and, as Roethke said himself, the one with the most obvious narrative construction. The poems preceding "The Lost Son" continue to test various lines of inner tension we have already noted in the protagonist. Sexual agony, lack of identity, and solitude are cast as barriers against the vital energy of the spirit in its evolution but with no lasting success. The closing portion of "O Lull Me, Lull Me" measures the spirit's achievement and attests once more to the protagonist's intuition of harmony with creation:

> I'm more than when I was born;
> I could say hello to things;
> I could talk to a snail;
> I see what sings!
> What sings!

Light, movements of air, flowing water, and the music of song supply Roethke with some favorite metaphors for these sudden revelations of increase and communion. And they are peculiarly appropriate and effective metaphors because their source is the great world of nature, which stands, as we have seen, as the foundation and setting for the poet's investigation of human reality. In Roethke's writing man is always viewed in the framework of nature, or at least is never far distant from it. Whether the immediate subject is the individual self, love between man and woman, or some kind of visionary experience, it partakes of that natural world in evident or indirect relationships, in the physical details of imagery. Finally, in some of his more recent poems such as "The Far Field," "Meditation at Oyster River," and "The Rose" Roethke sees the realm of the spiritual beginning in nature; yet he never denies the validity of the natural in favor of the transcendental. He tends rather to hold them in his vision simultaneously, for to his imagination they blend and interchange endlessly.

"The Lost Son," as Hilton Kramer wrote in his fine essay on Roethke, summarizes the main theme and the developments which appear loosely in the sequence as a whole. The first of the poems from this group we examined took the early phases of life as their point of departure, but here the reference to a cemetery in the opening line and the attraction to death which it signifies states at once the conflict with the evolving self whose pull is toward fulfillment and maturity. The remainder of this initial section, which is entitled "The Flight," treats the confused and often tormented condition of the child-protagonist as he tries to learn the direction he must take to escape those forces working solely for his anguish or destruction. In keeping with Roethke's preoccupation with the irrational and subliminal side of his protagonist's experience the poem assumes the strange aura of dream and fairy tale we have come to expect of the entire sequence. The protagonist undertakes his journey without certainty of his bearings or

24

his goal. All he can do, it seems, is ask questions and go where chance or the guidance of the spirit may lead him. The environment through which he travels (again we should stress the subjective character of his perceptions) displays hostility, though he has obvious feelings of sympathy for the smallest creatures, whose size and innocence resemble his own:

> At Woodlawn I heard the dead cry:
> I was lulled by the slamming of iron,
> A slow drip over stones,
> Toads brooding in wells.
> All the leaves stuck out their tongues;
> I shook the softening chalk of my bones,
> Saying,
> Snail, snail, glister me forward,
> Bird, soft-sigh me home.

As in previous poems from the sequence Roethke juxtaposes fragments of children's songs, nursery rhymes, and riddles with apparently factual descriptions; thus he keeps a balance between external and subjective reality. But even the fairly straightforward passages distillate a symbolic meaning in terms of the quest on which the protagonist is bound:

> Hunting along the river,
> Down among the rubbish, the bug-riddled foliage,
> By the muddy pond-edge, by the bog-holes,
> By the shrunken lake, hunting, in the heat of
> summer.

The river with its steady flow, suggesting progress, intensifies by contrast the image of frustrated and unrewarded searching by the protagonist near those places, holes and slippery mud patches, that spell out the dangers of regression and defeat to his odyssey.

In "The Pit," the second part of the poem which is only one stanza long, the seductiveness of a descent into the earth, a relinquishing of self to the dark body of the mother, becomes an active threat to the protagonist. But an inner warning, perhaps by the spirit, prevents him from succumbing to what I think we must call a strong death-wish or a refusal of any further hardships in the search for human completion:

> Where do the roots go?
> Look down under the leaves.
> Who put the moss there?
> These stones have been here too long.
> Who stunned the dirt into noise?
> Ask the mole, he knows.
> I feel the slime of a wet nest.
> Beware Mother Mildew.
> Nibble again, fish nerves.

The section following treats sexual agonies and alienation. Roethke builds up to a terrifying climax the tension between the protagonist and his surroundings. The short, terse lines which he handles so deftly are essential to the poet's creation of this climactic atmosphere:

> The weeds whined,
> The snakes cried,
> The cows and briars
> Said to me: Die.

But the full weight of the poem up to this point, which is brought to bear on the word "Die," is released in the next stanzas, and we suddenly realize that the protagonist has survived the worst of his trials. He finds himself at the calm center of a storm and recognizes that he is poised on the threshold of a new spiritual phase, of transformation and rebirth: "Do the bones cast out their fire? / Is the seed leaving the old bed? These buds are live as birds." Still more lines of conflict succeed these indications of change, but they terminate at last in a gentle apprehension of natural things, which is, in its turn, broken by an unexpected, violent flash of interior il-

lumination and a period of turbulence ending in the restoration
of the protagonist to the familiar climate of daily life.

The two concluding portions of the poem bring the protagonist home to his father's greenhouse and to an interval of waiting.
The boy's sensitive awareness of the existence of the roses he tends
and watches there ("The roses kept breathing in the dark. / They
had many mouths to breathe with.") should also be understood
to connote the self-recognition earned through his troublesome
journey. Like these flowers he enjoys a precarious and fragile state
of being; his scrutiny of their gradual response to the coming light
of day duplicates a perception of his own slow ascent from the
abyss of inner tensions:

> A fine haze moved off the leaves;
> Frost melted on far panes;
> The rose, the chrysanthemum turned toward the light.
> Even the hushed forms, the bent yellowy weeds
> Moved in a slow up-sway.

The stately, graceful quality of this stanza, contrasting sharply
with the clipped style of previous parts, leads us without disrup-
tion into the meditative attitude of the final section, in which the
winter landscape, bare yet enduring, mirrors in its stark forms and
objects the present condition of the protagonist. From this symbolic notation with its imagery of the "bones of weeds" and of
"light" moving "slowly over the frozen field, / Over the dry seed-
crowns, / The beautiful surviving bones / Swinging in the wind"
there comes a shift to the mind of the protagonist deeply immersed
in what has been happening to him. His mind also moves, but
"not alone, / Through the clear air, in the silence." The poem
closes with two stanzas reflecting the spiritual questions raised
by the boy's experience as recounted in the first three sections of
the poem and, presumably, in the other poems of the sequence
placed before "The Lost Son":

> Was it light?
> Was it light within?
> Was it light within light?
> Stillness becoming alive,
> Yet still?
>
> A lively understandable spirit
> Once entertained you.
> It will come again.
> Be still.
> Wait.

We can hardly fail to notice here a recollection of T. S. Eliot's *Four Quartets*, a series of poems which parallel Roethke's in some respects. Both works are explorations of the self, its past history and its developments, though Eliot has no intention of representing those prerational areas of the mind into which Roethke so daringly plunges. Both works seek realization in a spiritual order, but Roethke declines to step into religious orthodoxy and relies upon his own intuition, while Eliot integrates his mystical perceptions with the traditions and beliefs of Catholic Christianity. Yet Roethke's reference to the senior poet is too obvious to be merely an unconscious allusion. I think we should see it as a deliberate echo of *Four Quartets* but also as a statement of difference. The illumination which occurs in "The Lost Son" may be a divine visitation or a gift of grace; however, it lacks any explicit theological structure of the kind embodied in so many of the details in Eliot's poems. For Roethke this moment of light appears to be given as a matter of course and is accepted as completely natural. Certainly it is merited to a degree by the ordeal through which the protagonist has passed, but it surely is not achieved in the sense in which Eliot achieves those mystical experiences at the heart of *Four Quartets*, that is, by prayer, selflessness, and meditation. Roethke's is the more protestant approach, one that bases itself firmly on personal knowledge and evidence, on the lone individual's apprehension of the transcendent. And such a description applies to mystical poems like "In a Dark Time," which is as yet uncollected.

The purpose of this visitation at the close of "The Lost Son" is clear all the same, for it displays the progress of the spirit over the longest and most difficult stage of evolution. In the seven remaining poems of the sequence Roethke continues to record the advances and lapses of his protagonist, though we are by now conscious of the latter's increasing maturity. But he has not yet escaped the pains of sexuality and of alienation: they have become the problems of a person who has left childhood behind and arrived at a more comprehensive vision of himself and of the world around him. The poet even tells us the protagonist's age in the third part of "Praise to the End!":

> The sun came out;
> The lake turned green;
> Romped upon the goldy grass,
> Aged thirteen.

In spite of persistent obstacles passages of lyrical exaltation occur with greater frequency than they do in the poems preceding "The Lost Son." Such superior moments, with their pleasure in the beauty and variety of nature, look forward to some of Roethke's last poetry. Stanzas like the following from "I Cry, Love! Love!" (which takes its title from William Blake's "Visions of the Daughters of Albion") prepare the way for the vision of life we find in "The Far Field" or "Meditations of an Old Woman":

> I hear the owls, the soft callers, coming down from
>   the hemlocks.
> The bats weave in and out of the willows,
> Wing-crooked and sure,
> Downward and upward,
> Dipping and veering close to the motionless water.

A fish jumps, shaking out flakes of moonlight.
A single wave starts lightly and easily shoreward,
Wrinkling between reeds in shallower water,
Lifting a few twigs and floating leaves,
Then washing up over small stones.

The shine on the face of the lake
Tilts, backward and forward.
The water recedes slowly,
Gently rocking.

After the unusual and striking techniques which he introduces for his special purposes in the sequence poems, Roethke turns back again to a more formal manner in the early 1950's. In some of this work, most notably in "Four for Sir John Davies" and later in "The Dying Man," he makes use of cadences somewhat reminiscent of those in the poetry of Yeats, but these are intentional effects on Roethke's part and not, as some critics would have us believe, signs of weakness and of an unassimilated influence. Roethke ably defended himself against such charges in his essay "How to Write Like Somebody Else," pointing out that the poet needs to work forward consciously from his predecessors, that "the language itself is a compound . . ." And finally, he adds, "the very fact" that the poet "has the support of a tradition, or an older writer, will enable him to be more himself — or more than himself."

What Roethke says on this subject is profoundly true and is peculiarly applicable to himself. With his sequence finished he could no longer exercise the devices employed there: that vein was thoroughly mined and could only be kept open at the risk of repetition, boredom, and stultification. But he had learned a good deal from the sequence, and the themes which engaged his imagination were far from exhausted; in fact, one might venture to say that the exploration of the past, of personal history, served to make the present very available to him. The evolution of the self was not done, and the love poems begun during this period show that this evolution was entering a new, more expansive phase which related the self to the other, or the beloved. Technically speaking, Roethke tested the possibilities of a formal style, but with a daring, a liberty and passion that go beyond the urgencies of amorous feeling. His experiments in the sequence poems freed him to attempt an altered diction and looser syntax, more exclamatory, interrogative, and aphoristic lines:

> I'd say it to my horse: we live beyond
> Our outer skin. Who's whistling up my sleeve?
> I see a heron prancing in his pond;
> I know a dance the elephants believe.
> The living all assemble! What's the cue? —
> Do what the clumsy partner wants to do!

To get a better impression of the distance Roethke has traveled thus far in his poetic style, let us set next to those lines above from "Four for Sir John Davies" a stanza from "The Heron" in *Open House*. Though the rhythms of both passages are fundamentally iambic, the latter will call to mind the more restricted, tense character of the poet's first work:

> The heron stands in water where the swamp
> Has deepened to the blackness of a pool,
> Or balances with one leg on a hump
> Of marsh grass heaped above a musk-rat hole.

The piece which best prepares us for the considerable group of love poems now gathered into their own section of *Words for the Wind* is "Four for Sir John Davies," an ambitious poetic cycle that appeared among the last pages of Roethke's Pulitzer Prize volume of selected poems, *The Waking* (1954). As the title implies a little covertly, the basic metaphor of the poem is dancing. Roethke draws openly on two other poets to enlarge the dimensions of his poems: they are the sixteenth-century English poet to

31

whom these four pieces are dedicated and William Butler Yeats. From Davies' *Orchestra* (1594), a long philosophical poem on the harmonious relations of the various spheres of being in the universe, Roethke gains support for the cosmic scheme he includes in the first poem, "The Dance." But since *Orchestra* is constructed about a supposed dispute between Penelope and her suitor Antinous, who are dancing together, the sexual theme has also already been evoked, though as yet only indirectly. And it is to Yeats that Roethke looks for precedence in the treatment of sexual love through the figure of the dance, as well as for certain rhythms and qualities of tone and diction.

"The Dance" begins with the poet recalling the universal system to be found in Davies' poem, then questioning whether man any longer conceives of the world in terms of the dance within his own mind. Whatever the answer to that question may be, he affirms his own participation in such a cosmic dance and even humorously identifies himself with the shambling but pleasurable gait of bears:

> The great wheel turns its axle when it can;
> I need a place to sing, and dancing-room,
> And I have made a promise to my ears
> I'll sing and whistle romping with the bears.

But Roethke intends something more than mild self-mockery here, for the bears in their dance throw into relief the sheer physical aspect of existence — in the poet as well as in themselves: "O watch his body sway! — / This animal remembering to be gay." The poem carries this note into the third stanza with emphasis now placed on the poet's own isolated dancing. In spite of the elation accompanying this joyous, willed activity there is an incompleteness in what he does that can only be corrected by the appearance of the beloved. This beginning poem of the four closes with a stanza expressing Roethke's debt to Yeats:

32

> I take this cadence from a man named Yeats;
> I take it, and I give it back again:
> For other tunes and other wanton beats
> Have tossed my heart and fiddled through my brain.
> Yes, I was dancing-mad, and how
> That came to be the bears and Yeats would know.

ˣThe next poem, "The Partner," brings together the poet and his beloved in the dance. It becomes clear immediately that their relationship is more than sensual, more even than love between two persons, for overtly sexual gestures generate metaphysical overtones until we sense that Roethke attains a kind of visionary intuition of human possibility through his dancing lovers:

> Things loll and loiter. Who condones the lost?
> This joy outleaps the dog. Who cares? Who cares?
> I gave her kisses back, and woke a ghost.
> O what lewd music crept into our ears!
> The body and the soul know how to play
> In that dark world where gods have lost their way.

The "dark world" of which the poet speaks is undoubtedly the maze of love and bodily attraction. It may further imply the realm of the human, fully realized in the sexual and spiritual bond of the pair, as opposed to a supernatural plane of being altogether removed from life. We enter that world more completely in "The Wraith," where lover and beloved apparently exchange identities through their union. Though this poem aims specifically in its imagery and reference at the intense moment of completion in the sexual act, it extends past that in Roethke's speculations on the meaning of the act. Certainly we do not exaggerate in saying that he wishes to reveal the spiritual transcendence emerging from carnal love in the poem:

> There was a body, and it cast a spell, —
> God pity those but wanton to the knees, —
> The flesh can make the spirit visible . . .

33

The wraith, "a shape alone, / Impaled on light, and whirling slowly down," who is the poet's image of his beloved, is briefly associated with Dante's Beatrice in the first stanza of "The Vigil." In those lines Roethke asserts the purity of the lover's vision of the beloved. Created from his "longing" it may be contradicted but not destroyed by the reality of the loved one as a person. But the allusion to Dante and Beatrice goes further because it supports the transcendental experience recorded in the poem's last stanza, an experience which never denies the physical nature of the love relationship and yet presents it as the cause of a breakthrough in the spiritual order:

> The world is for the living. Who are they?
> We dared the dark to reach the white and warm.
> She was the wind when wind was in my way;
> Alive at noon, I perished in her form.
> Who rise from flesh to spirit know the fall:
> The word outleaps the world, and light is all.

Such a visionary climax is predicted by the similar but less comprehensive bursts of illumination in "The Lost Son" and other poems of that sequence. Even more important is the fact that moments of this kind recur throughout the love poems and again, of course, in the unmistakably visionary and meditative work that follows. It is necessary to understand first of all that Roethke's love poems are not just evocations of the beloved or descriptions of his aroused emotions with regard to her; these play their part in what he writes, but it is only one part. As I hinted earlier, this group of poems brings to a certain measure of fulfillment the evolution of the self begun with the childhood and adolescence poems. So Roethke tends to locate the loved woman at the center of the physical universe: through her he communes with that world and its elements, and has his vision transformed. Once more we think of the reference to Dante, of Beatrice's guidance which brings that poet to a revelation of the Divine. Surely the beloved in Roethke's poems, though she can change swiftly from a wraith-like to an earthy creature, functions in a manner closely resembling her predecessor. And perhaps it adds a little to my point if we also know that the woman to whom Roethke was married is named Beatrice.

A poem that is one of the most fully achieved as well as one of the most representative of the considerations discussed here is "Words for the Wind," which gives its title to Roethke's collected verse. Other of the love poems do take up various strands of the themes of death, spirit versus flesh, ultimate belief, and so forth, but they gain much more prominence in "The Dying Man," an elegy to Yeats, and "Meditations of an Old Woman." In a recent anthology, *Poet's Choice*, edited by Paul Engle and Joseph Langland, Roethke says that "Words for the Wind" was written as an epithalamion to his bride during their honeymoon visit at W. H. Auden's villa in Ischia, but these are merely the external circumstances of composition. The poem itself is literally a song of joy, a mood in the poet which arises from delight in his companion but overflows into the world outside. Perhaps it would be even more accurate to say that his love for this woman awakens and refines in him a knowledge of a participation in the life of creation, in the being of all things. His beloved merges with flowers, the wind, a stone, the moon, and so she appears to be present in almost every living thing, in objects or the elements. As the last line of the opening stanza intimates, he has the sensitive reverence for them we think of in a St. Francis of Assisi, who would make a particularly appropriate patron saint for Roethke's poetry:

> Love, love, a lily's my care,
> She's sweeter than a tree.
> Loving, I use the air
> Most lovingly: I breathe;

> Mad in the wind I wear
> Myself as I should be,
> All's even with the odd,
> My brother the vine is glad.

Not only does this love result in a harmony with the cosmos but it accomplishes an internal balance too. The self that was, so to speak, divided against itself in many previous poems arrives at unity through another person, a woman who is frankly physical and sexual but is furthermore a creature of spiritual and mythological proportions. In the intensified perception of the poem we see her continual metamorphosis, her changing roles, but at the same time she remains a constant image within the poet himself, the archetypal female principle dwelling in man which Jung called the *Anima*:

> The shallow stream runs slack;
> The wind creaks slowly by;
> Out of a nestling's beak
> Comes a tremulous cry
> I cannot answer back;
> A shape from deep in the eye —
> That woman I saw in a stone —
> Keeps pace when I walk alone.

In spite of this disclosure of a psychic image Roethke concentrates most of his imaginative powers on the external world and the forms of nature. The second section of the poem is devoted almost totally to natural imagery through which the course of love and the person of the beloved are traced. Here we find creation transfigured by the lovers who move within it and color it with their complex of emotions, "the burden of this joy":

> The sun declares the earth;
> The stones leap in the stream;
> On a wide plain, beyond
> The far stretch of a dream,

A field breaks like the sea;
The wind's white with her name,
And I walk with the wind.

Love in the figure of this woman "wakes the ends of life,"
Roethke tells us, and I do not believe it is misleading to say that
she and the poems about her suggested to the poet some of the ap-
proaches and devices of his later writing. "The Dying Man" and
"Meditations of an Old Woman," the two poetic cycles which
conclude *Words for the Wind*, are meditative and both employ
the persona or mask to obtain a more objective dramatization of
viewpoint.

At the start of "The Dying Man" the imagined voice of Yeats
alternates and blends with Roethke's through the five lyrics com-
posing it, and the style is itself a combination of the poetic speech
of the two men. This adaptation of the Yeatsian manner and mood
is not merely casual but quite intentional. In his late poems Yeats
was, of course, paradoxical, outrageous, and extremely powerful,
with a seemingly boundless reserve of energy to dispose to these
ends. He brought together spiritual and sensual modes of experience in unexpected, even sensational, ways and under the harsh
light of his irony. Roethke wished at times to use his poetry as
Yeats did, to probe the extremes of perception and knowledge
which the self may attain. "The Dying Man" is just such an imaginative effort; and the fact that it is both an elegy for Yeats and a
utilization of some of his language and techniques should not
prevent us from seeing how Roethke is really examining himself
and his own situation.

The opening poem, "His Words," records the message of "a
dying man / . . . to his gathered kin." This man is presumably
Yeats, and what he says seems an amalgam of the thought of Blake
and Yeats. Here the last stanza proves most influential in stirring

37

the mind of the poem's narrator (Roethke himself) to his own observations:

> "A man sees, as he dies,
> Death's possibilities;
> My heart sways with the world.
> I am that final thing,
> A man learning to sing."

The second poem begins with the revaluation of his life and work which these last words and the death following them force upon the poet-narrator. In addition, he feels the potentialities of existence revived: "I thought myself reborn." The subsequent stanzas range back over past experience, the poet's love and its opposite, the darkest moments of the spirit when he "dared to question all." A knocking "at the gate" announces most probably the presence of death, but the poet puts that off in the concluding line.

Three other poems, "The Wall," "The Exulting," and "They Sing, They Sing," make up the rest of the cycle. All of them reach beyond the bounds of a reasoned arrangement of ideas and perceptions in favor of a terse but ecstatic and visionary utterance. Themes are intermingled, but they include the poet's psychic burdens:

> A ghost comes out of the unconscious mind
> To grope my sill: It moans to be reborn!
> The figure at my back is not my friend;
> The hand upon my shoulder turns to horn.

and the fusion of natural and transcendental knowledge:

> Though it reject dry borders of the seen,
> What sensual eye can keep an image pure,
> Leaning across a sill to greet the dawn?

These passages, taken from "The Wall," both use the image of the sill as the apparent threshold separating the conscious self from the unconscious and from external reality. The wall turns up in the third stanza as the limit of what can be known, and thus the poet can recognize his dilemma as that of "a spirit raging at the visible."

"The Exulting" begins with a statement of the childlike innocence and freedom which once satisfied the poet but which now have aroused further yearnings:

> I love the world; I want more than the world,
> Or after-image of the inner eye.

Yet the most explicit account of the object of his desires, if it can be so described, is withheld until the final stanzas of the last poem. There nature asserts itself as a means of revelation for Roethke, and he has a vision of reality corresponding to the words of the dying man in the initial section of the poem — "Eternity is Now" — a vision that calls to mind Blake's famous passage from "The Marriage of Heaven and Hell": "If the doors of perception were cleansed every thing would appear to man as it is, infinite." The world gives the poet intuitions of the eternal and the infinite through its temporal, finite creatures and things — if he has learned how to see or has been granted this frightening clairvoyance:

> I've the lark's word for it, who sings alone:
> What's seen recedes; Forever's what we know! —
> Eternity defined, and strewn with straw,
> The fury of the slug beneath the stone.
> The vision moves, and yet remains the same.
> In heaven's praise, I dread the thing I am.

The poem's ending lines, of great strength and beauty, set forth the loneliness and uncertainty but also the singular determination of the poet in his confrontation of the unknowable or the void where the Divine may be sought. Roethke furnishes no answers and, as he does elsewhere, keeps within the strict confines of his personal perceivings:

> Nor can imagination do it all
> In this last place of light: he dares to live
> Who stops being a bird, yet beats his wings
> Against the immense immeasurable emptiness of
>   things.

"Meditations of an Old Woman," a longer and superior group of poems, consists of several dramatic monologues spoken by an aging lady, modeled on the poet's mother, who muses on her past, on the meanings of an individual's existence, as she faces the prospect of death. Over and above those poems included in the collected edition and in the volume of light verse (which also reprints the so-called greenhouse poems) *I Am! Says the Lamb* (1961) there are a considerable number of later poems which so far have been published only in reviews and magazines. Roethke planned a book for them, completing it shortly before his death; it had not yet appeared at the time of this writing. While space permits no discussion of the very late poems here, it ought to be said that they take the manner and technique of the "Meditations" as their starting place. Some of them become even looser in form; some are fragmentary, explosive, and epigrammatic; some turn to a taut lyricism. Many are shaped by that mixture of description and reflection so prominent in the "Meditations." Through these poems runs a continued fascination with ultimate questions of mortality, God, the final significance of human life. Of course these are questions about the self too, and they constantly bring Roethke's evolutionary theme to its highest level, that is, to occasions of visionary knowledge. But if we cannot go further into the as yet uncollected poems in this essay we should look at "Meditations of an Old Woman," both as the foundation of later work and as the last part of *Words for the Wind*.

The "First Meditation," which inaugurates the series of five poems, offers the reader opening stanzas that create a harsh mood of old age, winter, frailty, and severely restricted expectations. We can capture something of the ominous quality of this section from the initial lines:

> On love's worst ugly day,
> The weeds hiss at the edge of the field,
> The small winds make their chilly indictments.

Thus the title and the beginning provide us with the personal situation from which the speaker's memories and thoughts are set in motion. As Roethke so frequently does, he expresses the condition of a person's life through happenings or objects in nature. The old woman's recognition of death is conveyed vividly by external events: "stones loosen on the obscure hillside, / And a tree tilts from its roots, / Toppling down an embankment." And here we must remember that it is *her mind* which entertains these images of sliding stones and falling trees.

In spite of the temporal erosion that has worn away the speaker as though she were a thing exposed to wind and dust and rain there is an essential life of the spirit preserved in her described by Roethke as "light as a seed." Small that life may be, but it has a toughness and resiliency which enables it to burst forth with a vigorous assertion of its own being. The effort of the spirit to be renewed is characteristically reflected in careful details of the actions of nonhuman creatures, a fish, for example:

> So the spirit tries for another life,
> Another way and place in which to continue;
> Or a salmon, tired, moving up a shallow stream,
> Nudges into a back-eddy, a sandy inlet,
> Bumping against sticks and bottom-stones, then swinging
> Around, back into the tiny maincurrent, the rush of brownish-white water,
> Still swimming forward —
> So, I suppose, the spirit journeys.

41

This passage could be seen as a paradigm of the five poems, for the old woman's meditation, which spans the period of time in the poetic cycle, is analogous to the rest enjoyed by the salmon before he renews his journey against the stream. For precisely this brief duration we are allowed to enter the speaker's mind and witness her thoughts.

Within her consciousness, as might be expected, there are alternating currents of imagery and ideas. Her attention may shift rather abruptly from past to present, from the actual to the speculative, from knowledge to dream, as we would naturally imagine it to do readily in a person of advanced age who has a lifetime to think upon and its termination to face. Yet whatever these fluctuations of consciousness might be and however random they might seem at first glance, all of them contribute to a pattern of repeated affirmations of life which reach a peak of lyrical strength at the end of "What Can I Tell My Bones?"

In contrast to this pattern the poems also contain the elements of despair, evil, and nothingness: all that thwarts the steady forward movement of the spirit. One could, in a more comprehensive study of Roethke's poetry, draw up two lists, of his positive and negative imagery, and not simply for the poems under discussion but for his work in general. We have already noticed some of the recurring metaphors and symbols in passing. Most of them will be familiar to the reader who has watched the texts with care. On the positive side we find spring and summer; the sun and moon; small creatures of the bird, insect, and fish variety; wind and flowing water; flowers, plants, and grass. On the negative side would appear winter; aridity; still and muddy waters; holes, pits, or caves; dust; desolate landscapes. The old lady in her reflections also must countenance the memory of negative experience, if only to defeat it. In the following lines we can see how she conceives

42

the life-denying by bringing it together in her mind with the life-giving and the sacramental:

> I have gone into the waste lonely places
> Behind the eye; the lost acres at the edge of
>   smoky cities.
> What's beyond never crumbles like an embankment,
> Explodes like a rose, or thrusts wings over the
>   Caribbean.
> There are no pursuing forms, faces on walls:
> Only the motes of dust in the immaculate hallways,
> The darkness of falling hair, the warnings from
>   lint and spiders,
> The vines graying to a fine powder.
> There is no riven tree, or lamb dropped by an eagle.

Like D. H. Lawrence, with whom the critic Kenneth Burke once very interestingly compared him, Roethke locates a substantial moral vocabulary in the natural order. Perhaps these uses are not intentional in every case of such imagery, but certainly his images very often serve a purpose of the kind I have named.

The moments of ecstasy in these poems, as elsewhere in Roethke's previous work, tend to occur through the life of nature or within its boundaries. "I'm Here," the second of the "Meditations," is largely devoted to memories of the old woman's girlhood years: from them arise scenes of an innocence, an awakening of flesh and spirit in concord with the surrounding world:

> I was queen of the vale —
> For a short while,
> Living all my heart's summer alone,
> Ward of my spirit,
> Running through high grasses,
> My thighs brushing against flower-crowns;
> Leaning, out of all breath,
> Bracing my back against a sapling,
> Making it quiver with my body . . .

43

And again:

> The body, delighting in thresholds,
> Rocks in and out of itself.
> A bird, small as a leaf,
> Sings in the first
> Sunlight.

The closing poem compels the speaker once more to encounter the forbidding prospect of a slow crumbling away to death; yet it is at last her love for all things, especially the commonplace or simple things of which our everyday world is made, that urges her back from somber meditation to the flow of existence. The tired, aging lady with whom the cycle of poems began emerges from shelter as if life had just been given her by an "agency outside . . . Unprayed-for, / And final." But Roethke is not explicit about this agency as yet. Later, uncollected poems such as "In a Dark Time" recount the poet's experience of God in trance-like visions. The emphasis in the "Meditations" falls upon earthly possibility, the self's embrace of the entire horizon of existence open to it:

> The sun! The sun! And all we can become!
> And the time ripe for running to the moon!
> In the long fields, I leave my father's eye;
> And shake the secrets from my deepest bones;
> My spirit rises with the rising wind;
> I'm thick with leaves and tender as a dove,
> I take the liberties a short life permits —
> I seek my own meekness;
> I recover my tenderness by long looking.
> By midnight I love everything alive.
> Who took the darkness from the air?
> I'm wet with another life.
> Yea, I have gone and stayed.

Few contemporary poets can match the daring, the richness, and the freedom — which is really to say, in summary, the beauty — of

44

these lines. It is too soon after Theodore Roethke's sudden death to sit in any final judgment on his work — indeed this essay was written while he was still a vital part of the literary community. But surely the intensity and clarity of Roethke's vision in addition to his tremendous lyrical force and technical ability place him, as John Crowe Ransom has recently said, in company with some of the finest modern American poets, a company which includes among its members Wallace Stevens, William Carlos Williams, and, I should like to submit, E. E. Cummings. His art shows the poet's desire to extend himself, to try his skill and imagination, and his growth was organic and true. Roethke's sense of direction was bold and challenging yet unfailingly accurate. The metamorphoses or transformations through which he and his poems passed in the last decades are caught in the old lady's words near the end of "What Can I Tell My Bones?" What they tell us of that speaker, her aspiration and strength, they also tell us about Roethke and the magnitude of his poetic accomplishment:

> The wind rocks with my wish; the rain shields me;
> I live in light's extreme; I stretch in all
>   directions;
> Sometimes I think I'm several.

✗ Selected Bibliography

Works of Theodore Roethke

POETRY

Open House. New York: Knopf, 1941.
The Lost Son and Other Poems. Garden City, N.Y.: Doubleday, 1948.
Praise to the End. Garden City, N.Y.: Doubleday, 1951.
The Waking: Poems 1933–1953. Garden City, N.Y.: Doubleday, 1953.
Words for the Wind: The Collected Verse of Theodore Roethke. Garden City, N.Y.: Doubleday, 1958.
I Am! Says the Lamb. Garden City, N.Y.: Doubleday, 1961.

PROSE

"Open Letter," *Mid-Century American Poets,* edited by John Ciardi. New York: Twayne, 1950. Pp. 67–72.
"The Teaching Poet," *Poetry*, 79:250–55 (February 1952).
"Last Class," *College English*, 18:383–86 (May 1957). (Written under the pseudonym Winterset Rothberg.)
"How to Write Like Somebody Else," *Yale Review*, 48:336–43 (March 1959).
"Some Remarks on Rhythm," *Poetry*, 97:35–46 (October 1960).

Current American Reprint

Words for the Wind: The Collected Verse of Theodore Roethke. Bloomington: Indiana University Press. $1.75.

Bibliography

Matheson, John William. *Theodore Roethke: A Bibliography*. University of Washington, Master of Librarianship thesis, 1958.

Critical Studies

Arnett, Carroll. "Minimal to Maximal: Theodore Roethke's Dialectic," *College English*, 18:414–16 (May 1957).
Bogan, Louise. "Stitched in Bone," in *Trial Balances*, edited by Ann Winslow. New York: Macmillan, 1935. Pp. 138–39.

46

Burke, Kenneth. "The Vegetal Radicalism of Theodore Roethke," *Sewanee Review*, 58:68–108 (Winter 1950).

Kramer, Hilton. "The Poetry of Theodore Roethke," *Western Review*, 18:131–46 (Winter 1954).

Kunitz, Stanley. "News of the Root," *Poetry*, 73:222–25 (January 1949).

Lee, Charlotte I. "The Line as a Rhythmic Unit in the Poetry of Theodore Roethke," *Speech Monographs*, 30:15–22 (March 1963).

Mills, Ralph J., Jr., "Roethke's Garden," *Poetry*, 100:54–59 (April 1962).

———. "Theodore Roethke: The Lyric of the Self," in *Poets in Progress*, edited by Edward B. Hungerford. Evanston, Ill.: Northwestern University Press, 1962. Pp. 3–23.

Ostroff, Anthony, editor. "The Poet and His Critics: A Symposium on 'In a Dark Time,'" *New World Writing*, 19:189–219 (1961). (This includes short essays by John Crowe Ransom, Babette Deutsch, and Stanley Kunitz, and a reply by Roethke.)

Rosenthal, M. L. *The Modern Poets: A Critical Introduction*. New York: Oxford University Press, 1960. Pp. 240–44.

Schwartz, Delmore. "Cunning and Craft of the Unconscious and the Preconscious," *Poetry*, 94:203–5 (June 1959).

Southworth, James G. "The Poetry of Theodore Roethke," *College English*, 21:326–38 (March 1960).

Spender, Stephen. "Words for the Wind," *New Republic*, 141:21–22 (August 10, 1959).